Poems for Ruth

By Alan Mitchell

First published in the United Kingdom in 2024 by
The Choir Press

ISBN 978-1-78963-512-6

Author's note

You sit at the roadside watching the traffic of your life go by. Everything passes you, including yourself. Nothing is permanent. But poetry is an alchemy, which transforms experiences and memories and fixes them (through words and images) in their time and place, as the poet's challenge to impermanence.

Contents

Tigers

You kiss me,
Then do things to my hair till it is right.
You touch my face,
Then miss me with your eyes though you are looking.
Love's my last belief.
Tap the window if you feel that it's a bore –
My last belief.
You look away at me – again I feel unsure,
So I retreat.
What now of talk of sensitive perceptions –
I do not care.
What now of talk of sensitive perceptions –
I think of Tigers.
Now it seems I'm on my last belief
And where my heart is
I seek the vision of the Tiger's pace
And beauty in its face
Replacing you who do not seem to care –
Beautiful face
Let the tangle of my mind become your stalking place.

Quirigua

On a road in Guatemala,
Skin in soft cotton
Connects in a road rhythm
Of accidental tenderness –

No words are spoken.

Your hand alights on my arm,
Gentle as a mariposa
(A pretty name for a butterfly)
I turn and your face is happiness –

No words are spoken.

At Quirigua the Maya left silence
To fill a thousand years
We add to the silence, which soaks us
Like sweat on soft cotton –

No words are spoken.

At Camus's grave

Sitting in the sun in Lourmarin,
Time is paused in "lizard moments".
Triangulated and transfixed as one
We say nothing, but feel we belong.
Absurd, or not, after thirty years
This is the constant we have known.

Happiness Lost

Happiness was mine once,
Then I lost it long ago,
But memory, an image of a smile
Implies I had it then.
Was I young,
Or was it yesterday?
Time deludes and warps my recollection,
Of when I lost my happiness.
Perhaps I'll find it soon, perhaps,
But not if what they say is true,
That it depends on state of mind.
For if that's so I fear it's gone,
My mind's near empty,
I just looked
And couldn't find there anything,
But pictures of a broken heart
Arranged on walls of very black
And echoes of a stupid laugh
And yet, I'm almost sure,
Happiness was mine once.

Sisyphus and I

He smiles,
Watching his fate
Roll away.

Sardonically, he says,
"I won't follow",
But does.

No illusions
His choice
Truth hurts
But not yet.

He reflects,
Reaching respite
In memories.

The sun sets,
Soft gold
Salving his senses.

Descending
His shadow lengthens.
Then darkness falls
As his fate awaits.

By Plockton

Again I'm on a beach of coral corpses,
Fossil relics snap beneath my feet,
Rendered frail by aeons of abuse,
My tread confirms destruction with each step.
In this I read a metaphor for life
We tread a path and never give a thought
To whom we stand on as we make our way
Towards the vision of our precious self.

Someday

Someday,
Come that certain season,
A season when the climate's wrong,
Between the gaze of helpless eyes.
Will I make destruction call,
Although the inner echo sighs too late.
Will you be broken long,
Deposed of villa status,
Undressed of adoration,
I cannot think so.
You'll swim the shallow stream again,
The stream I almost drowned in.
Someday,
Under the sneer of sunny skies,
I'll leave this dreary town,
Cultural anus of the western world,
Not in defeat but in its victory,
Will I strike out to find my world too late.

Who's taller?

October sun like rare wine
Spills its last on moving trees,
Casting dark stains on white light grass
In shifting contrasts changing fast.

But we the still witnesses
Ignore all presence but our own
And hold our sweet communion
Expressed in closeness and in touch.

I give you my attention
As you press to my open shirt
The gift of broken flowers
That you have gathered for my love.

I hold you then, we do not move,
Until a passing man arrives
And stops to say some simple words
Then fades into the dappling,
I watch him wondering why?

Words fail us

Sun trapped we are silent,
Words are sacrilege,
As face to the sky
We worship quietly.

Love's afterglow is when words fail us –
Dante said.
All is touch and sensual silence
When the sweetness flows.

For the rest it's talk,
Talk, talk, talk, talk,
With nothing said –
Nothing of meaning.

Words aim high but fall away
Into the verbal abyss,
So always trust the senses
Not the interlocutor.

Waiting

Animals are machines without souls,
Thought a clever Frenchman in a stove.
A gift from God for us to abuse.
But your fate is worse,
As you sit there waiting.
Fretting at tissues –
(Confusion's confetti)
Covering your feet,
While all you have left is waiting.

Then the last day comes
And rain turns to sun.
You touch wet roses
And their perfume touches you.
I kiss your forehead
And then I am gone.
Soon you are gone too,
Putting an end to your waiting.

Poem for Jet

The problem is the meaningless other
Subtracting from life,
With each day less to subtract.

The idiot beside me distracts me
Tapping his foot to the musak,
Each tap subtracts me.

Jet was in the sun
Then he was dead.
Essentially, that's my memory.

I thought of "Futility",
"Gently its touch awoke him once",
"If anything might rouse him now",
I thought of blasphemy.

Assume I could escape,
The arithmetic of less
Is there anything left to say –
Anything?
Or am I an echo already,
Deluded – metaphorically dead –
Subtracted by the meaningless other?

Fragments of loss

Love is such a fragile longing,
So hold on please don't drift away
Or time will lose us in its passing
And make of us a memory
And we in turn will drift in turn
Into a dream that passes hours
In which our love will live again
In all its dead intensity.

Our life is a bad dream,
A dream through which we're falling,
Tumbling down in silent anguish,
Never landing always falling,
Dropping through life,
Silent, calling.

Why, everything's a question once more,
When life past living aches in the void
That is you.
Substance, resonance, emptiness, dissonance
Echo the agony, rebounding, resounding
Use up the cavity
That is you.
Why, is everything cheaper once more?
Worthwhile becomes less, sane becomes shame
In exquisite pain
That is you.

Going Nowhere

Cheap nights, cheaper illusions
Going nowhere like you
And this sweating stranger
Sweating for him not you.
Waiting for some kind of goodness
Chance might make an eternity.
Gambling for some kind of joy
Creating a sweeter reality
That won't be yours tonight.
So your loss is his gain,
As you focus your tired eyes
Upon this heaving humanity,
Now reaching embarrassed oblivion
While choking back his lies.

"Horse"

Then there was a pause
Dilated to eternity
In your eyes.
Like flying saucers some might say
(Unkind perhaps as a simile)
Moving closer to eternity
Like your eyes
When in repose
Before brief tears arrive
To then disclose
That everything in life is gone but this,
To help you to and from your degradation.

Smiling Irony

Once I watched a woman love me
And what her heart contained she said she gave to me
And in return I gave to her my poverty
My lack of wealth but more my lack of love.
But she, like me, indifferent to her dignity
Placed all her trust upon a futile hope,
So now and then I'd slip from objectivity,
Into a state of mind of grudging awe
That she who got so little gave so much
Might cause my mouth to grin I liked the irony,
Expressed in giving so much wasted trust.
Now she has left and someone watches me
And what my heart contains I give to her,
But now and then I long for objectivity
That slipped from me into another time,
So that I'm left to place my hope in trust
And trust that hope will always be enough,
To win for me the continuance of my sanity
Now I am also prey to smiling irony.

The only reality

The search for meaning
Is a meaningless quest,
So sometimes we rest,
Rest in the moment.
These moments
Of brief elation
Confirm our only reality.

The tool shed

What a waste of time you were
For both of us.
I was out for destruction anyway.
He saw it –
Mother's son –
I saw he saw it,
His beaten blue eyes told me so.
But I couldn't forestall it.
I'm a bastard I suppose –
My Mother's son.

The earth in that box is years old,
But the weeds are new.
Dating earth is such a thankless task,
Like appealing to bastards I'm told.

Father and son

Is this my long recovery,
A few short lines of poetry
To someone I love?
I'm sorry to embarrass you,
I know you'll cringe at love.
Yet once you held my hand in yours,
Hardly a manly thing to do,
So can't I be forgiven too, for love.
From all the past that shines through,
When once you held my hand.
I felt like a young girl at a dance,
Who couldn't believe her luck,
Being held by someone she was totally there for,
As I was there for you.

Introduction

Nature hopes for nothing,
Because it doesn't need to.
It fulfils its own promise in spring,
Then kills it without malice in winter.

Poem

You would stay if I would let you,
But you do not bear fruit anymore.
So, this is an end of season day,
A day to wear something against memory,
Of forgotten warmth and lost fecundity.
I might feel a twinge of remorse, of loss,
Something intangible, somehow irrational,
But nothing lasts for ever – that's rational.
And today is a rational day,
To take you away, throw you away
And think of another season.
When another will flower and fruit for me,
To be consumed through a summer till –
You would stay if I would let you,
But you do not bear fruit anymore.

Token grief

One gone and one to go
And still the humor flowed.
You won't be dead until you die
And being dead you'll never know to cry,
But I will cry for me –
Fear prompts in us this show.
And while you live and hobble through my mind
I'll cry for us Rimbaud.

Emptiness

Emptiness, nothing fills up everything,
Expanding time till bursting point is breached,
When nothing flows releasing nothing,
So, pressure on time from nothing grows.
Sadness fills my heart with emptiness.
How strange is nothing causing pain.
That negative can be so positive,
That empty hearts their beats retain.
Emptiness, nothing fills up everything.
Everywhere it seems is silly paradox.
For how can nothing displace something,
Yet faith is nothing moving mountains.

Silver blade

I've thought about you silver blade,
So incisive so decisive.
I've run my finger down your edge
And watched slight pressure leave me red.
Then laid you in your plastic tray
And made it through another day.
Then thought about you silver blade
And how perhaps you'd suit my purpose.
When it's just down to you and me
And I'd still have your certainty.
So incisive so decisive,
My moment of reality.

Funchal

Hearts beat, time passes,
Night in a hotel room.
Outside a crane fishes in a silver pool,
Catching nothing but the light of the moon.
Inside, the ocean transforms to an angry gale
And the ceiling is by Wassily Kandinsky –
"White rectangle with black line orbited by its trapezium".
A voice asks, "Are you ok?"
My hand is held then disengages.
Hearts beat, time passes.
Sleep ends the illusion.
The canvas is black.

Howarth

Relics, unconvincing small,
Emily's dress or Charlotte's finery.
Tubercular frailty on riven frames.
Filigree gentility, swathed in claustrophobic finery.
Garments, as pretty winding sheets.
Hidden skin, translucent alabaster,
Blue veined epi-marbled filigree.
Cool, dark, dank beneath their finery,
Secret skin temperate for death.

Should snow baboons melt with the snow

Three Primates, noisy baboons,
Troup through snow and trees,
Crashing through alien landscapes,
Monkey people are we.
I, me, leader of three
Am followed by ageing female,
And brat baboon not mine,
Am male in rosy arsed prime.
Grubbing, we brush against trees,
Disturbing snow lichen filigree,
Drifting down through the breeze,
Soundless to hole the snow,
While we crash on aimlessly.
Sounds descend by size,
Volume ascends through the youngster,
Who screeches, that it is cold,
While the female barks for order
And the old male not so old,
Breathes broodily far up ahead.
Grubbers with fullest bellies,
We are but pseudo baboons.
Part time nomads, out for the day,
As likely to melt and fade away,
As the filigree that whitened the trees
And sun blistered now drips through the breeze
And threatens our future, we simian three,
Should snow baboons melt with the snow.

Mayan creation myth (adapted)

Before the "dawn" footsteps were there,
Warmed by the rising sun,
Then she approached and stepped in
To trigger the passage of time.

She walked through creation in forty days,
The backdrop she once belonged to,
Before her engagement with time
And the march towards eternity.

The burden of time is a gift,
If you believe in the constancy
Of your future found in the past –
The predictability of history.

That everything is set in the order,
Of footsteps through days,
Walked through a lifetime.
Each carrying their burden,
Till death slips the load to another,
Who steps in the footsteps,
As if from the start,
As if from 12Oc the first footsteps.

The burden of time is a curse,
Where there is no constancy,
But life lived in a rush.
Each competing with time,
To rack up the score of things done,
Before the burden's laid down.

Each playing the game for themselves,
As there is no shared continuum,
Only the paranoid race –
The absurdity of competing with time
Which hastens our footsteps to death.

At dusk Nature seems so still,
A tranquil memory walked away from,
Years ago, when those footsteps fell.

Now, as then, when the sun rises
I pick up the burden of time
And embark on another day,
Counting off my world in footsteps.

Peter

We drift through our days,
Routine to routine,
Breakfast to bedtime,
Sleep to wakefulness.

He died in obscurity,
Where most of us die.
Some words were said,
Some songs sung,
Then he was dead.

I had to write,
Hopeless or not,
To reach out
So, our minds might meet –

Watching white horses,
From Kaikoura beach
And the brooding backdrop
Of snow-capped peaks.

Driving dark canyons
Towards fading gold light.
Watching long shadows,
Not talking but sharing.

A song is playing
"Whatever's written in your heart?"
It touches us,
Without our saying.

You read my letter
Again and again.
Our minds met in memories,
"That's all that matters".

Lewis Pass (NZ)

Diminished
To a speck
On the forest floor
I wondered at the brightness –

Of the luminous moon
And luminescent stars.
The closeness of infinity.
The proximity of awe.

I sat by the river,
Tracking mist
Through trees.
Translucent threads,
Undone by the sun.

I listened to water
Impeded by rocks,
Gushing and noisy
Restless and angry –

Then I was drifting
Melted to torpor
By the sun's
Sleepy warmth.

But darkness appeared
Ending my reverie,
So I wound with the river
Towards Lewis Pass.

"Character is fate"

I stumble in a snow filled gulley,
Breathless and thirsty.
Finding a trickle of melt water,
I drink it greedily.

In the clear air and glittering snow
Is a scene of transformation,
A tiny miracle of rebirth
Where some Crocus grow.

Their yellow flowers
Pulse vividly,
Seem hallucinatory,
Under the Cretan sky.

I watch the open flowers
Straining towards the sun,
Filling their cups with warmth
While releasing the scent of saffron.

Gravel burns on my cheek
Take me back to the summit,
Where spread-eagled by the wind
I raged against indifference.

It wasn't fear that drove me,
It was apoplectic hate.
I wanted to kill the wind,
I wanted that as my fate.

Beyond this sound

Night surrounds.
There's nothing lonelier,
Now the creep of the sea crawls to shore –
A tired hush.
Not desperate to repeat itself,
But bound to rush.
Released from the trough of decision,
Unlike us.
Each time released by time the same sad hush,
Just like us.

Sun

Sun the stress of life is on you.
The Incas fashioned wonders with your tears.
Tears, you shed in gold, from which they made,
In worship, symbols of their veneration.
And hid them not in temples there to dim,
But placed them in the open that the source,
Of light reflected from the parent eye,
Should mingle with a pool of its own tears,
Remade by man into a new creation,
That somehow seemed to form a mystic link,
Between the Incas and their living God.

The supplicant who petitions humbly

When the sun shines I see my shadow,
A companion who is comforting.
Unlike the black void in my outline,
Which is the mirror of my death.
No shadows cross the threshold,
Just your presence and deafening silence.
I watch myself walk from room to room,
Then I fall to my knees – sanity riven.
Arms outstretched, my hands face upwards.
I say "please" to nothing, as no one is there.
I am the supplicant who petitions humbly,
For respite that cannot be given.

Mentor and nemesis

A man stuck an axe in my head.
This is reconstruction,
That is what he said.
Or was it mutilation,
For the rest of my life.
A reminder from my mentor,
That time is short
And death impatient.
A reminder from my nemesis,
That idleness has a cost.
The mirror will tell you,
Work hard from now on
For mentor and nemesis
Before you are gone.

The weight

The weight
Sits on my chest
Crushing my heart
With emptiness.

The sun is warm,
It scents the grass.
The breeze is gentle,
I think of you.

Sun's shadows
Casts a memory
Of darkness
As you walked away.

But you will come
And we will meet
To lift the weight
Of our defeat.

One day we'll learn
The weightless truth
That in our hearts
Beats victory.

Apparently

Words conceal what the world reveals.
Look and see, see and you will learn
That you are only part of the illusion.
But that's ok, that's all there is.
No things in themselves.
No ideal forms, no gods.
No meaning.
What you see is reality,
Not some three-card trick
Called religion
Promoting the eternal essence,
While disguising human ingratitude
Because the world is never enough.

Searching for certainty

A man waits in his cell of salt,
Staring at a screen for a glimpse,
A passing trace of Dark Matter
To appear from outer space.

In a quiet church a man waits,
Holding a bible in his hand,
Searching the words on a page,
Looking for a trace of his faith.

In a silent temple a monk waits,
Eyes closed to the painted veil,
For the death in life of Nirvana,
His distraction from the real.

Beware the semblance of something,
What you see might be a mirage
And the desert you cross,
Trying to get there,
Are just barren days of despair.

People disappear around corners,
Something compels me to watch.
Death is around the last corner,
You are there then you are not.

We appear, then we're gone –
Continuum unruffled.
That is the sum
Of every life,
Since time dawned
On consciousness
And Nature was lost.

The Sound of Ruth

She laughs a little at his silly game,
But shouldn't laugh, she knows she should remain
Denying that she heard him call her name,
Whispered down the wisps of her light hair,
In gentle breath forming in her ear,
A sound that echoes through her as her name,
And makes her laugh then squeal the word "again".
Anticipating lips upon her hair,
That touch at each strand gently with a sound,
The sound of Ruth that carries to her ear,
A sound that echoes through her as her name,
And makes her laugh, then squeal the word "again".
Then whisper in her laughing voice, "again", "again", "again".

The hanged mouse

In the half dark
You were there,
A medieval image
Of self-sacrifice.
You looked peaceful,
Eyes closed above comic whiskers,
Head resting to one side.
I slipped your noose,
Imagining your struggle,
Without rhyme, or reason,
Or fairness to it.
My sadness increased.
Why had you died,
Such a cruel death,
For a paltry pittance of seed.
Paying for your crime,
In medieval kind.
I said no prayer,
When I laid you to rest.
But my heart was with you.

Altitude lost, I gained Spring

From a cliff
I saw enchantment.
A scented paradise
Of small pink flowers,
Daphne, I think –
The water nymph.

In an emerald meadow,
Pulsating green,
I watched the crystalline cord
Of a narrow stream
Catch sunlight in its twisting.

A snake flashed at the speed of illusion,
So, was it really seen?
Shimmering green and yellow,
As it scythed across the meadow.

Shaded places hid Cyclamen,
Made known by their smell of honey.
And the fragrance of pine was whispering
Along the delicate wind.

Birds would sing,
Then be silent.
Fly, then be still
Like me.

I worship without faith,
Without measurement,
Without denial.
I worship what I see,
Not what can't be seen.
So, at times like these
I feel I've found reality.

The Forge (An Teallach)

A slight breeze makes it seem
Mountains sigh now and then,
But he is the only one there,
Silent as his shadow.

Thought leads inward to her
And a memory of her dying,
Of him gently bathing her eyes,
The last time he touched her alive.

Boots slip on shattered rocks,
Rending the total silence,
That and his angry cry,
Cursing his clumsy fall.

He watches his silent shadow,
Which is always just ahead.
And there it always will be,
The eternal trick of the sun.

Then his shadow crumples,
He watches it lean on his stick,
Rocked by his feelings of sorrow,
Reflecting his despair.

Eastward of his shadow
Sunrise splits the sky.
Mutely he stands and stares,
At the dawn of another day.

His tears mean more than words,
Droplets suffused with gold,
He thinks of Inca imagery –
The mythic "Tears of the Sun".

A wry smile is his saviour,
As he turns away from the light,
Toward his waiting shadow
And the Forge beyond his sight.

The Sumatran Rhinoceros

She is tiny for her kind,
The singer of her sadness,
Her song calls to a mate
Who is not there.

The silent forest hears from her
The sound of Nature dying,
But cannot help,
As it shares her ill-starred fate.

Instinct is her innocence,
Her simple beauty.
She cries because she must.
She cries to save her kind.

But she will die unheard,
She and her forest home.
As we destroy Nature,
Until all its beauty is gone.
Leaving an endless wasteland,
Where all that's left is our ugliness.

The Ice Axe

When doubts arise to dash resolve.
When thoughts confuse and hopes recede.
And images of love are blurred,
To dreamlike outlines by time obscured.
Wear this charm upon your breast,
A talisman of our love and hope.
Silver hard against skin so soft,
Resting upon such a gentle slope,
In a setting of perfect harmony.

Fishing (1)

I was a fisherman then,
Not a trawler type not quite,
But I'd fish for anything in anything,
Just me my rod and my loneliness.

I fished to get away,
But took it all with me
And pondered many a riverbank
Seldom thinking of fish.

Cold days of no success
Staying close to the earth,
Is how I remember my life,
When I was a fisherman then.

Fishing (2)

In riverine leafy bowers,
A Constable facsimile,
A subject out of time,
I'd stand with prop in hand
And pose for many hours,
Almost watching anything
That passed my half-cocked gaze.

But mostly I just sensed,
Especially the constancy
Of wet hypnotic rhythm.

Inhabitants came near,
Ducks and Coots and Voles
And sometimes fish would rise,
Pink throated speckled Trout,
Unattainable in their element,
That lapped against my boots
And made me think of fishing.

But mostly I just sensed,
Especially the constancy
Of wet hypnotic rhythm.

Fishing (3)

I stopped!
A moments admiration,
Chilled imagination,
Cold as your blood,
Checked that fatal cast,
That might tempt your cannibal brethren,
To leave their green gloom world.

I watched!
Your pierced back seep
Living liquid pigment,
In red striations daubed on gold,
Without regret.

I knew it then
That I could kill,
Fish or men,
It makes no difference
To cannibal brethren like us.

But had you screamed,
Or had your screams been heard,
It might have saved your life
And ended my complacency.
But you chose to quiver silently
And meet your savage fate.

I cast!
And moments later
Watched you – spellbound –
Swallowed by a Pike.

Still

A rabbit, there and gone
Trod the stillness silently
Leaving traces in memory
Of wind upon fur spiralling,
Then it is still.

A woodcock, breaking cover,
Slashes through the air
Careering like a drunken pilot
Ending his career,
Then it is still.

A Roe, bedeviller of sight,
Tells all eyes its lies
Merging then emerging
Seen and then not seen
Mirage of the forest,
Then it is still.

Nature is so still,
But creatures moving
Obscure the source,
The eternal scene unmoving,
That keeps it still.

Forever is a long time

Nothing is or can be known,
Guessed at, yes, but never known.
My hopes are built upon despair
And yet I believe in belief in something.
I have no God, but I have you
And for you I know I must deify life
And for you I know I must deify love,
Because your hope is less than mine
And because your belief in believing in something
Died with the hurt of times now past.
Hurt that makes you laugh at forever
And thoughts that love can last that long,
Although you wish it could be so,
Caution makes you cling to pain
That's scarred you with a cynic's view,
Which you must teach this naïve child.
You feel it's only right to say,
What you believe, but wish wasn't true,
That life can only be a hell,
With one or two good interludes.

Reduced

Car headlights – neon snowflakes in slow procession,

Passing sight – glazed in numbed reverie.

Mind blank – held receptive to suggestion,

Images close – imprinting lights configuration

On senses drained.

Tired joy flickers and dies,

As images recede, passing into dark recession.

Homecoming

How do we speak these days?
I have to silence my heart
To answer that.
And read appropriate poets for a clue,
To convey my love to you.
It seems one must aim for restraint,
Your heart won't break so don't say it,
No one is your world so don't think it.
Say "I prefer you to being alone",
"Our equipment fits so I'm happy when we screw",
Just make it droll so it sounds new.
So, when I arrive,
Don't come into my arms
And don't let me hold you near.
And please restrain the welcome of a tear,
Your heart might break, but don't say it.

Waiting and hoping

Life is the journey, time is the road
And you are stuck in loneliness,
Hoping to find the way,
To a place called happiness.
Your need to depart is urgent,
You want to leave loneliness soon,
But "soon" might never arrive,
So, departure is less than certain.

Then you are in a nightmare,
Of never finding the way,
From loneliness to happiness,
So, in loneliness you'll stay.

The path

Some days are complete,
Such days are flawless.

Some days banish thought,
Such days are seductive.

Some days last forever,
Such days are for the senses.

Some days give you everything,
Such days can be addictive.

Some days you are your senses,
Such days they surround you.

Some days you meet on a path,
Such days can beguile you.

Some days you embrace in the sun,
Such days are full of tenderness.

Some days are days of love,
Such days were part of us.

Some days are held in memory,
Such days will never pass.

A memory

Many times I have held you,
In satin soft moments of birth
When from sleep's womb we were thrust
Into the vortex of another busy day.

Our eyes closed, refusing to open
We lived blind, like small creatures
Advancing by sense of touch alone,
Till the light insisted on wakefulness.

Then our eyes met and with a smile
Lips moved close to close on lips
Across the downy landscape.

Invisible walls

Separation is a heartless road
Taken by many fools,
Who build invisible walls,
From layers of doubt and hate,
Cemented with resentment,
When love and trust are lost.
Invisible walls are a paradox
They only exist in the minds
Of builders without forgiveness
Or memories of better times,
Of quiet moments and the need
To simply say I love you
And share the human warmth
That can breach invisible walls.

Meconopsis

We hold the moment
My blue friend and I,
As we have stopped time
And captured the present,
Which we have made still
Along with my mind.

Looking into your flower,
I see more and more
The intricate details
Of pale green and blue
And dark green and violet
Lit by silver and gold.

Rivers and tributaries,
Veins lit by the sun,
Flow through your leaves,
Edged with bright hairs,
That look strangely aberrant
And not of your world.

A dark creature in shadow,
With a long curving tail,
Looks up to your flower,
At stigma and stamens,
Green girdled with gold,
And plots his desire.

A room of human concepts

The white walls oppress me
With their pristine purity,
Reflecting isolation
And defining the room.

Which is not bare,
Should you believe
Human concepts
Are there.

Self-contained,
Preceded by nothing.
Non-interactive,
Beyond understanding.

There, in each corner
Of a six-sided room
Alone and inert
With access denied.

I am aware of an odour
The smell of old certainties,
So, I open the window
On the natural world.

On Reality before Time
And God were invented.
And Meaning, Knowing and Being
Were entangled as one.